THE EARLY YEARS OF
RHYTHM & BLUES

THE EARLY YEARS OF
RHYTHM & BLUES

Focus on Houston

By Alan Govenar

Photography by Benny Joseph

Rice University Press
Houston, Texas

Copyright © 1990 by

Alan Govenar

All rights reserved

Printed in Japan

1990

Requests for permission

to reproduce material

from this work should

be addressed to:

Rice University Press

Rice University

Post Office Box 1892

Houston, Texas 77251

Library of Congress

Catalog Card

Number 89-43407

ISBN 0-89263-273-9

CONTENTS

ACKNOWLEDGMENTS

In producing this book I am especially grateful to Benny Joseph, whose attentiveness and insight guided this work to completion.

I am also thankful to the following people who offered their assistance and encouraged me to proceed with my efforts: Patrick Stewart of the Amon Carter Museum, Ron Gleason of the Tyler Museum of Art, John Wheat of the Barker Texas History Center, Daniel P. Davison, Jr., of Documentary Arts, Inc., William Ferris of the Center for the Study of Southern Culture at the University of Mississippi, Alvia Wardlaw of the Dallas Museum of Art and Texas Southern University, Robert E. Galloway of the African American Heritage Museum of Houston, Roger Armstrong and Ray Topping of Ace Records in London, and Ron Evans, who provided diligent counsel and skill in the printing of the photographs.

My work on this book was supported in part by grants from the Texas Commission on the Arts, the Cultural Arts Council of Houston, and the National Endowment for the Arts through the Southern Arts Federation.

The Early Years of Rhythm & Blues

ALAN GOVENAR

THE EARLY YEARS OF RHYTHM AND BLUES
ALAN GOVENAR

"Everybody wanted to get out, to go to the music—gospel in the churches, rhythm and blues in the city. The wages were low and the music talked to the people." So says award-winning bluesman Johnny Copeland, recalling the Houston of his youth in the 1950s. He goes on to explain, "There were hardly any televisions and only two black radio stations, KCOH and KYOK, but dances were held on Monday, Thursday, Friday, Saturday, Sunday, and sometimes Wednesday at the Eldorado Ballroom, Club Matinee, Diamond L Ranch, Club Ebony, Shady's Playhouse, Double Bar Ranch, and Club Savoy."[1]

Eldorado Ballroom
Houston, late 1940s
Courtesy Houston
Metropolitan
Research Center
Houston Public Library

On weekends, music events and dances were held day and night and after hours. KCOH and KYOK had remote broadcasts from grocery stores, automobile dealerships, and talent contests, and they sponsored concerts at the Negro Home Show and the City Auditorium. Teen dances were held at the black high schools—Jack Yates, Phillis Wheatley, and Booker T. Washington—weekly at the Eldorado Ballroom, and at the YWCA. Segregation was institutionalized in Houston but was beginning to weaken. Martin Luther King, Jr., Thurgood Marshall, and the civil rights movement were a focus of hope in the struggle against racism and bigotry. The activism and energy of those years were reflected in rhythm and blues music and documented in the photography of Benny Joseph. Through his images of musicians, dances, recording sessions, concerts, and day-to-day life, a picture emerges of the Houston African American community in which rhythm and blues developed and flourished.

Rhythm and blues differs from the blues form that preceded it. The phrase "rhythm and blues" was introduced in 1949 in *Billboard* magazine as a substitute for the word "race" in a chart that had been labeled until then "The Top 15 Best Selling Race Records."[2] "Race" was a catchall for any kind of African American recording and had been in use since 1920, when the record "Crazy Blues" by Mamie Smith spawned the recording of blues music.[3] After World War II, the connotations of "race" became offensive and "rhythm and blues" came to reflect changes in race relations and black music in general. The new music was a creative response to the realities of inner-city ghetto life, urban migration, and social protest. The most important influence in the shaping of rhythm and blues was gospel, which contributed form and style.[4]

In rhythm and blues the twelve-bar form of country blues is replaced by the eight- and sixteen-bar patterns of gospel and popular song. The instrumentation of early rhythm and blues is characterized by an interplay of shouting vocals or soulful ballads with electric guitar, saxophone, piano, and drums. In Texas, rhythm and blues developed a distinctive sound that derived from Aaron "T-Bone" Walker, whose performance style combined an exuberant stage presence with a mastery of the electric guitar.[5] Walker introduced the electric guitar as a lead instrument that superseded the saxophone. He had learned about it from fellow Texans Eddie Durham and Charlie Christian, who had pioneered its use as a rhythm instrument in jazz.[6] The guitar style of T-Bone Walker was decidedly different from earlier styles and meshed jazz-tinged chordal changes with fleet single-string arpeggio runs. Mariellen Shepphard, who grew up in San Antonio during this period, remembers seeing T-Bone Walker often in the 1950s and says he was unforgettable.

"I was sneaking off on maid's night out. So I was up there as close as I could get and T-Bone comes out in his white suit with big diamond rings. He comes out there and strikes up his guitar, v-room, v-room. Oh, Mister T-Bone! He couldn't even get through the first song before the purses started flying and everyone going, 'Play my song, Mister T-Bone. Take all my money,' and he was so cool. But then after he got hot, he'd put that guitar behind his head. Then he'd start plucking [those strings]. He'd turn around and swing, and then everything went: shoes, rings, bracelets, everything. Honey, he'd play them blues all night long. But sometimes the

T-Bone Walker, 1942
Guitarist with Milton
Larkin Orchestra
Chicago, Joe Louis'
Rhumboogie Club
Milton Larkin Collection
Courtesy Houston
Metropolitan Research
Center
Houston Public Library

men got mad at the girls for throwing their money and purses or whatever else they could on stage. T-Bone would come back out and start playing again, and they threw anything they could get loose."[7]

T-Bone Walker epitomized the idiom of rhythm and blues, and he had a profound influence on the electric guitarists who followed him, including Johnny Copeland, Joe Hughes, Pete Mayes, Roy Gaines, Clarence Green, ZuZu Bollin, T.D. Bell, Blues Boy Hubbard, and BB King, as well as their white successors, Duke Robillard, Ronnie Earl, Jimmie Vaughan, Stevie Ray Vaughan, Anson Funderburgh, and Johnny Winter.[8]

In the 1950s Houston emerged as a center of rhythm and blues. Many African American musicians were native to the city and many others came from East Texas, Arkansas, and Louisiana. The major record companies of the day sent recording scouts to Texas, and in Houston several independent labels were started to compete in the growing market for local talent.[9] Of the independents, Peacock Records was clearly the most prominent.

Gatemouth Brown
Promotional photograph
Houston, 1950s
Courtesy Hans Kramer

Peacock Records was founded in 1949 by Houston businessman Don Robey to record Clarence "Gatemouth" Brown, a headliner at Robey's Bronze Peacock Club. Robey had opened the Bronze Peacock in 1946 as a restaurant and music showplace for T-Bone Walker, Louis Jordan, Ruth Brown, and the other rhythm and blues and big band stars of the day. Evelyn Johnson, Robey's longtime business associate, recalls, "The Bronze Peacock attracted a mixed audience, black and white. Different companies and social clubs had parties there. We had the finest food and chefs. We couldn't sell anything to drink, but people could bring their own bottle. We sold set-ups, and they could drink until midnight. Then we had to pick up everything."[10]

Eddie Mesner of Aladdin Records frequented the Bronze Peacock whenever he was in Houston, and in 1947 he signed Gatemouth Brown to a recording contract. Robey acted as Brown's manager and flew him to Los Angeles, where later that year he recorded four sides for Aladdin, including "Gatemouth's Boogie" and "Guitar in My Hands." Robey, however, was dissatisfied with the release timetable, and when Aladdin failed to renew the option in Brown's contract, he decided to start the Peacock label.[11] Evelyn Johnson remembers, "Don said, 'We don't need the Mesners. We can make our own records.' I said, 'We will?' and he replied, 'Oh, yes.' I asked, 'How do you go into the record business?' and he answered, 'Hell, I don't know. That's for you to find out.' Well, we went from there on a more serious note.[12]

"Anytime we didn't know something, I'd call up some record company and ask questions. I'd telephone the major labels, and when they wouldn't talk to me any more, I'd try someone else. I even called the Library of Congress, and if they couldn't answer my questions, they'd refer me to this or that person. There were so many details to learn about copyright, publishing, union scales, and musician fees. I'd contact the Harry Fox Agency to get information I knew was not handled by his office, and the secretary would say, 'Why don't you try so and so?' and I did."[13]

Initially, the offices of the Peacock label were located in Robey's record shop at 4104 Lyons Avenue but were later moved to the Bronze Peacock at 2809 Erastus Street. Of the five sides Robey recorded with Gatemouth Brown using the Jack McVea Orchestra, "Mary's Fine," backed with "My Time Is Expensive," became a regional hit. Records were pressed on order, and distribution was a slow process.

Robey's biggest early success came with the gospel recording "Our Father" by the Five Blind Boys of Mississippi. Of lead singer, Archie Brownlee, gospel authority Tony Heilbut writes, "He would demolish huge auditoriums with the bluest version of the Lord's Prayer and would interrupt his songs with an unresolved falsetto shriek that conjured up images of witchcraft and bedlam."[14] Music historian Arnold Shaw credits Brownlee with introducing the scream that became the hallmark of soul music.[15] The recordings of the Five Blind Boys of Mississippi were followed by a series of gospel releases on the Peacock label featuring the

Gospelaires of Dayton, Ohio, the Dixie Hummingbirds, the Sensational Nightingales, the Mighty Clouds of Joy, the Reverend Cleophus Robinson, and the Bells of Joy.

Don Robey was a well-known entrepreneur and a reputed gambler. He was born in Houston in 1903 and rumored, because of his light skin, to be of Negro, Irish, and Jewish descent. Robey was a self-made man, an avid hunter who carried a gun and had bodyguards. He was feared for his aggressiveness and temper, but respected as a promoter and record producer.

In his day-to-day operations Robey depended heavily on Evelyn Johnson. From 1950 to 1967, she managed the Buffalo Booking Agency, which promoted Robey's recording artists, cultivated new talent, and also represented musicians like BB King and Albert Collins, who were independent of Peacock Records. Evelyn Johnson observes that as a booking agent, "I was mother, confessor, lawyer, doctor, sister, financier, mother superior, the whole nine yards. What they needed they asked for, and what they asked for they got."[16]

"She was one of the great women of her time," says BB King. "I don't think she gets enough recognition, because to me she was one of the pioneers. She helped lots of people, not only in the blues field, but in jazz, soul, and what became known as rock music."[17]

The first rhythm and blues singer with whom Robey made the *Billboard* charts was Marie Adams, whose song "I'm Gonna Play the Honky Tonks" was a hit in 1952. Later that year Robey expanded his

Johnny Ace
Promotional photograph
Houston, 1950s
Courtesy Huey P. Meaux

Bobby Bland
Promotional photograph
Houston, late 1950s
Courtesy Hans Kramer

recording interests by acquiring the Memphis-based Duke label from WDIA disc jockey James Mattis. Through this acquisition Robey gained the rights to the musicians who were then under contract to Duke, including Earl Forest and the Beale Streeters, a group that featured Bobby Bland, Rosco Gordon, and John Marshall Alexander, Jr., who recorded as Johnny Ace.

Johnny Ace had several hit records before his death in 1954, including "My Song," "Cross My Heart," "The Clock," "Please Forgive Me," "Saving My Love for You," and "Never Let Me Go," although his greatest national acclaim came with the posthumous release of "Pledging My Love."[18]

Bobby Bland was in the United States Army when Robey bought the Duke label, and after his discharge in 1955, he renewed his contract. Between 1957 and 1970, Bland had thirty-six songs on the Duke label that reached the *Billboard* rhythm and blues charts. Among his bestselling records were "Further on Up the Road," "I'll Take Care of You," "Call on Me," "That's the Way Love Is," and "Turn on Your Love Lights." *Cash Box* magazine named him "Rhythm and Blues Artist of the Year" in 1961.[19] Bobby Bland says, "Robey gave every artist the benefit of the doubt starting out. Robey was a regular businessman. It was the business that caused people to have all kinds of vibes about him. He was a hell of a man, and he was a help to a lot of black entertainers who would never have gotten a record label at all. Houston at that time was a blooming city."[20]

During the 1950s, Robey traveled around the United States in search of new talent, and musicians in turn pursued him with the hope of being discovered. Willie Mae "Big Mama" Thornton began making records for the Peacock label in 1951 after Robey heard her sing at the Eldorado Ballroom in Houston with an Atlanta troupe known as the Hot Harlem Review. Her initial releases on Peacock, "Mischievous Boogie" and "Partnership Blues," were recorded with Joe Scott's band but did not sell well. Thornton's first song to make the *Billboard* charts was "Hound Dog," produced by Johnny Otis while she was touring in California in 1952 and not released by Robey until the following year. For fourteen weeks in 1953, "Hound Dog" was number one on the charts but was limited in distribution, like other black recordings of the period, because of its status as a rhythm and blues song. In an interview with Arnold Shaw, Robey comments, "In those days rhythm and blues was felt to be degrading, low, and not to be heard by respectable people."[21] However, when "Hound Dog" was re-recorded by Elvis Presley in 1956 for a white audience, it became a nationwide smash hit. Big Mama Thornton continued to record for Peacock but left the label in 1957 because of a dispute with Robey over money.

Among the other recording artists under contract to Robey were Joe Hinton, Buddy Ace, O. V. Wright, and Herman "Junior" Parker. Junior Parker signed with Robey's Duke label in 1954, although his first song to make the *Billboard* charts was "Next Time You See Me" in 1956. Over the next decade Junior Parker had several hits on the Duke label, most notably "Sweet Home Chicago" in 1958, "Five Long Years" in 1959, "Driving Wheel" in 1961, and "Annie Get Your Yo-Yo" in 1966.[22]

Robey's success in the record industry owes much to the writers, arrangers, and instrumentalists he gathered for sessions in Houston, Chicago, and elsewhere around the country. The sophisticated big band arrangements, intricate T-Bone Walker-styled guitar phrasing, and brassy orchestral flourishes organized by Joe Scott, Joe Fritz, and Bill Harvey led a wide array of session musicians (Paul Monday, Hamp Simmons, Grady and Roy Gaines, Clarence Holloman, Johnny Brown, John Browning, Pluma Davis, Wayne Bennett) to create what became known as the Duke/Peacock sound. Robey is reported to have disliked "downhome" blues, such as the kind performed by Sam "Lightnin'" Hopkins—consequently, little of this material appeared on the records he produced.[23]

In addition to Duke and Peacock, Robey owned the Lion Publishing Company and also started the Songbird and Backbeat labels. He even recorded a few white singers, most notably Roy Head, whose song "Treat Her Right" was a hit on the *Billboard* charts. At the peak of his career in the 1950s and 1960s, Robey had more than one hundred artists and groups under contract to his labels, and over the course of a single year he used as many as five hundred studio musicians. Robey's business began to wane in the mid-1960s, although he benefited from the influx of British rock and roll and the revival of interest in rhythm and blues. In 1973, when a court decision in litigation with Chess records went against him, Robey sold Peacock Records and its subsidiary labels to ABC/Dunhill on the condition that he remain as a consultant, which he did until his death in 1975.

The Robey years in Houston constitute an important period in the

Willie Mae Thornton
Houston, 1950s
Courtesy Huey P. Meaux

Joe Scott
Houston, 1960s
Courtesy Huey P. Meaux

Roy Head

Houston, 1960s

Courtesy Huey P. Meaux

history of the city and in the growth of American popular music. As a black entrepreneur in the white-dominated recording business, Robey was confronted by numerous obstacles. The problem, Evelyn Johnson says, was twofold: "First, we had to find people to sell the records, we produced, and then we had to put up the money to get airplay. What we were asking the disc jockeys to put on the air, the station managers were telling them not to. Racial discrimination was everywhere and we were geographically situated wrong. Houston was not the mecca of the industry, but that also worked to our advantage to some extent. That's why we were able to operate the way we did. For so long, who cared about us? The major companies were in New York, and they didn't pay us any attention until it became clear that we really were going to compete."[24]

To protect his interests Robey insisted that his musicians sign exclusive agreements, and he used an alias — Deadric Malone — to share authorship of many of the songs his company recorded. "This was a legal transaction that was standard practice," Evelyn Johnson says. "He purchased a share of the copyright. There were people who sat around the office and wrote lyrics. Joe Medwick was one of the best. He'd sit in the reception room and write five or six song lyrics in a day. He'd written ten the night before, and he'd bring them and Don would buy all of them for five or ten dollars each."[25]

Many musicians distrusted Robey's business practices but nonetheless benefited from the cash advances, automobiles, clothes, and musical instruments that he lavished upon them. Evelyn Johnson maintains that Robey was "a fair businessman with his musicians. Don Robey was as good as he was bad. He was Dr. Jekyll and Mr. Hyde. Very few people in this world knew Robey. I did. He gave them everything they could possibly want and that was his mistake. So many of the musicians never realized or took into consideration that some of this money had to come back. In reality, he hardly recouped what he put into a lot of them, but when their money didn't come up, they decided he was taking advantage of them. What money? They had already spent everything they had coming to them.[26]

"The Peacock years were remarkable," says Johnson. "Music had a different place in people's lives. We made a special kind of history in spite of what people say. What we were doing was different. Some said we didn't play blues. Well, everything we did wasn't blues, but we had to fight this little battle with those who didn't approve of what we were doing. We had that big band swing sound, and consequently we never got our just dessert. We were part of what was called the 'Chitlin' Circuit'. It was a downgrade thing. With integration it was a little easier to get our records out and to get airplay, but the major companies didn't approve of our independence. Peacock was one of the last independent labels to be sold. I never knew why we were called independent when we were the dependent one."[27]

Written accounts of the growth of Peacock Records are scant. Because of the controversial nature of his business practices, Don Robey was private about his dealings and affairs.[28] Some of the most enduring documentation of Robey's personality and the legacy of Peacock records, aside from the music itself, is photographic. From the beginnings of the record company and the Buffalo Booking Agency, Benny Joseph was contracted to photograph musicians, recording sessions, and promotions.

Benny Joseph with his Speedgraphic camera Houston, 1950s Photograph by Herbert Provost

In addition he made studio portraits for many musicians in Houston. The importance of photography in building Robey's record business cannot be underestimated. Not only were the photographs essential to advertising and promotion, but they provided a lasting historical record. "There weren't that many photographers around," Benny Joseph recalls, "and when they needed some pictures, they'd look for a commercial photographer. I was just one that Robey chose. I used to do a lot of things for him. On job promotions he'd call me to take pictures of different dances and entertainers. He used to go hunting and he'd come back with a bunch of deer tied over his car. Well, he'd call me to come out and take pictures of them."[29]

Benny Alvin Joseph was born in 1924 in Lake Charles, Louisiana, and moved to Houston at age two with his mother after the death of his father. He worked professionally as a photographer in the African American communities in Houston from 1950 to 1982. His interest in photography began in 1940 while he was a student at Jack Yates High School. After his discharge from the army in 1945, he enrolled in a two-year program at Teal's School of Photography, then affiliated with Houston Junior College for Negroes (which later became Texas Southern University). A.C. Teal was a prominent black portrait photographer who prepared his students for careers in commercial photography.

From 1950 to 1953, Joseph shared a studio at 1806 Dowling Street with a fellow student, Herbert Provost. In 1953, he moved his darkroom to his home, where he worked until 1958, when he opened a studio at 3505A Wheeler Street. To supplement his income during this period, Joseph also worked as a nursing assistant at the Veterans Administration Hospital. Joseph says, "From 1953 to 1959, I worked the midnight shift, twelve midnight to eight o'clock in the morning. Then I'd do photographic work all day. At the hospital I helped with the psychiatric patients. They'd howl all night long. Around 1955, the hospital began giving them thorazine to help them sleep and I was able to sleep a little bit myself. But one day they said they were going to put me on the day shift. So I resigned and decided to devote myself completely to photography."[30]

**Benny Joseph's
Speedgraphic camera
Houston, 1988
Photograph by
Alan Govenar**

In 1968, Joseph moved his studio to 2305 Blodgett Street, where he stayed until he retired.

Joseph's studios were utilitarian. "In the studio I painted the walls a bluish color," he says. "I also had rolls of paper that I could unfurl as a backdrop. I did portrait sittings, display sittings, anything I had to shoot. I had a darkroom with a Beseler condenser enlarger and an Elwood enlarger. Then I had a room for retouching negatives, a room for drying prints, and a room for stamping the finished prints with my name."[31]

For portraits in the studio during the early years of his career, Joseph used a Speedgraphic 4x5 camera with four lights: "a main source, a fill-in, a highlight, and a backlight."[32] Generally, his portraits were head shots, although musicians, he indicates "often wanted a full body pose which showed their musical instruments and style of performance. They were aware of the power of the photograph in the shaping of their

Benny Joseph's
workspace and
enlarger
Houston, 1988
Photograph by
Alan Govenar

public image." When the photographs were distributed, the photographer was rarely credited; he or she was paid a flat fee for producing a set number of prints, which were in turn mass produced and given away for nothing.

On location, Joseph "used my Speedgraphic and flashbulbs. Someone would call me and they'd tell me for what event they wanted me on assignment. Then I had to try to get some idea of what they were looking for. And it took me a long time to figure that out, because at first I used to make a lot of pictures and people would say, 'Well, this doesn't have news value. Why didn't you take it this way or that way?' Then I began to learn what made a good news picture, and I tried to capture that. I used to ask the people, 'What do you want?' And they'd set up their scene, whatever scene they wanted, and that's what I'd shoot, nothing else. I never did shoot much on speculation. I charged twenty-five dollars for an assignment and five-fifty for a print, but it was understood that I owned the negatives. I was furnishing the film and all the supplies. The only prints I made were the ones people requested, other than of course what I did for my family and friends. I always used a cream-colored, fiber-based paper. The black tones were deeper and more subtle, especially when selenium toning was used for permanence. Toning altered the coloring slightly. I put a lot more into my printing back in the 1950s than I do now, but I didn't save any of the prints for myself."[33]

Among African Americans in Houston in the 1950s, photography was considered a trade or vocation, not an art form.[34] Like his contemporaries Louise Martin and Herbert Provost, Joseph had to "do it all" to make a living as a photographer—portraits, snapshots, news, advertising, churches, parades, politicians, dances, and musicians. Although studio portraiture was the mainstay of Joseph's business throughout his career, he also worked for the local chapter of the National Association for the Advancement of Colored People (NAACP), KCOH radio, Peacock Record Company, Buffalo Booking Agency, and other local businesses.[35] His main concern as a photographer was making a living to support his wife and family. This involved hard work and long hours.

The photographer in the black community was a respected businessman whose presence was valued at social occasions but who was supported largely through studio work, negative retouching, and printing. In discussing the work of Benny Joseph and other black

Benny Joseph in his
attic darkroom
Houston, 1988
Photograph by
Alan Govenar

Jimmy Nelson before
retouching
Houston, n.d./535
Photograph by
Benny Joseph

Jimmy Nelson after
retouching
Houston, n.d./535
Photograph by
Benny Joseph

photographers of his generation, art historian Alvia Wardlaw explains that in the 1940s and 1950s blacks "needed to project a very positive image of themselves. Their photographs were not found in the larger, white-owned Houston newspapers but were published only in black-owned publications, the *Houston Informer* and later the *Forward Times.* The photographs were essential vehicles for maintaining a positive sense of self.

"When you look at Joseph's photographs, you want to comment. He's capturing the repartee that you hear. There's the sense that he just jumped in and did it."[36] The people he photographed—at teen hops, high school proms, coronation balls, social club dances—were self-conscious about their appearance but recognized the importance of the photograph. There is a formality to a lot of the pictures that reflected the "very polished image that photographers were able to provide to people. Physical dignity was especially important during the period of segregation. Those kinds of images were the bread and butter for black photographers."[37]

Joseph says, "The biggest challenge was taking pictures of people over age thirty-five. They'd see the proofs and say, 'I don't like that. It doesn't look like me.' They didn't want to look their age. Some didn't like their hair, their nose, their lips, their wrinkles. So, I'd tell them about retouching." Joseph recalls, "I had the motto, 'Where there's beauty, we take it; where there's not, we make it.' Retouching negatives was very important. Teal was good at retouching, and he taught me how to etch negatives. People wanted the blemishes and imperfections removed, and that's what I did."[38]

For black high school seniors, the class portraits had particular significance. Of her years at Yates High School, Alvia Wardlaw recalls, "Getting your yearbook and going to the prom were major events, but your class pictures and ring were even more important. For many students that was *graduation,* because they were going to work at the post office or in various other jobs that were available for black high school graduates. There weren't that many of us who would be going on to college. Graduation was an incredibly strong tradition that the entire family became involved in—grandparents, aunts, and uncles who had been at Yates were at commencement."[39]

Graduation from high school was a rite of passage, and the photograph and the ring were signs of affirmation. People used to dress up for their class pictures, according to Wardlaw, as if they were going to a school assembly. On assembly days, "the girls couldn't come to school bare-legged. They were sent home if they didn't wear hose or socks, and the young men looked almost like businessmen. They wore coats and ties and carried attaché cases. There was a kind of determination the students felt during the beginning of the civil rights period. There was a very strong sense that we were being prepared for something more than just furthering our education. You were being prepared for life. What it meant to be a young black in the 1950s and 1960s was embodied in the photographs that were taken at that time."[40]

Even for those who quit school before graduation, the studio photographic portrait was significant. For blues singer and guitarist Joe Hughes, the photograph, "marked the achievement of my new status as a professional musician. I had grown up in the Fourth Ward until I was three or four, and then we moved to the Third Ward. I went through the high seventh, lower eighth grade. My mom had died and I really started playing my music. I quit school because, from the crowd response, I just felt that I could make it from there. I was good with my hands and could play the electric guitar. There was no problem getting work. At that time we played practically for nothing because we loved to play. My first job I think I made a dollar and a half, me and Johnny Copeland, and all the beer we could drink, but we didn't drink.

"Everything was beautiful to me at that time because I loved the music so much. I loved to see people having fun. Most of the black clubs were small then. A lot of houses were converted into clubs. That gave you basic two- or three-room structures, but there were so many of them around the city. People frequented their favorite clubs and were relaxed around each other. They really knew how to enjoy themselves back then. People today seem to be geared more toward work. Back then you weren't making enough money to get rich so you didn't worry about it. You hoped that you made enough to enjoy yourself.

"The 1950s and 1960s were the greatest for the music. You have so many electronic things today that it's taken the purity away from it. People felt the music more back then because the music was about them. And the musicians played with more feeling. Those little clubs would be jumping, and soon the bigger clubs opened, like the Eldorado Ballroom and Shady's Playhouse in the Third Ward, the Club Matinee in the Fifth Ward, where they had talent contests and live radio remote broadcasts on KCOH. Lyons Avenue was to the Fifth Ward what Dowling Street was to the Third Ward. The Eldorado was at Elgin and Dowling, Club Ebony was on Rosewood and Dowling, Club Savoy was on Wheeler and Dowling, and Shady's Playhouse was on Elgin and Ennis. During those years everyone was closer together."[41]

Segregation in Houston affected all aspects of life. "It was around you," Alvia Wardlaw remembers. "You knew what it meant from an early age. You encountered it in the grocery store. There was a colored water fountain and a white water fountain. Every adult in the community made you aware of segregation and discrimination, but at the same time you could forget about it when you were doing things that were part of your community, like going to the games and pep rallies, or hearing civil rights activists like Barbara Jordan or the Reverend William Lawson speak."[42]

Desegregation in Houston proceeded slowly and came as a result of bitterly fought legal battles.[43] During this period Benny Joseph was sometimes called to photograph the evidence of discrimination and racism. He says, "I worked for the black civil rights attorneys Francis Williams, George Washington, and others as well as for Carter Wesley, publisher of the *Houston Informer*, the NAACP, and the PYA [the Progressive Youth Association]*."[44]

Many of Joseph's news photographs were published locally in the *Informer*. One, however, gained national attention—a March 1960 photograph of Felton Turner, an unemployed awning installer. Turner had participated in a sit-in with Texas Southern University students and was followed home by four masked white youths. The youths abducted him at gunpoint as he walked through the Heights and took him to a deserted wooded area not far from downtown Houston. There they strung him up in a tree, beat him with chains, and carved two sets of KKK initials on his abdomen with a pocket knife—but they didn't kill him. Joseph says, "Carter Wesley sent me out to take pictures of the man. He wasn't hanging; he was out of the tree, and I went to his house. The pictures were published in the *Informer*, and about a month later they appeared in magazines around the country. Carter Wesley had sent them out."[45]

*A "direct action" group involved in protests against segregated public accommodations in the 1960s.

As a photographer, Joseph himself sometimes experienced discrimination. "One time," he says, "I wanted to take some night pictures downtown. I set up my camera on Main Street, and I was taking a time exposure when a police officer walked up. He asked, 'What are you doing?' I said, 'I'm taking a picture.' And he said, 'You can't take any pictures around here.' So he made me fold my tripod up, but I had already made my exposure by then. I had a time shot of about six seconds and he talked a lot longer than that. He didn't know if I was taking a picture or not."[46]

On another occasion, "they had a bunch of sit-ins in jail downtown, and one of the civil rights bosses wanted me to take a picture of them getting out. The police were going to let them out at a specific time. So I was down there with my camera waiting and I saw that a lot of people from the general public were going to the police cafeteria to eat. I said to myself, 'Well, I'm going to take a picture of this because the city had been saying the cafeteria was only for police personnel.' So I threw the door open and flashed a flash with my Speedgraphic and quietly walked away. And the proprietor came out and asked, 'Who took that picture?' But I didn't say anything and he never did find out. I think he was too nervous and he went back into the cafeteria. Well, a little while later, when the civil rights sit-ins were released, the proprietor came out with a bunch of hamburger steaks and fed them all for free. That was in the early 1960s, when they were trying to desegregate, and he was afraid that the cafeteria might become the target of further protest."[47]

Most public accommodations were integrated in Houston without violence between 1960 and 1965 as a result of the sit-in movement and the Civil Rights Act of 1964. Desegregation and court-ordered integration, however, generated new problems for Benny Joseph and many other black entrepreneurs. "Most of my work from 1950 to 1968 was school pictures," Joseph says, "but by 1968 things had changed. Integration killed that. The white principals wouldn't hire me."[48]

KCOH disc jockey Skipper Lee Frazier observes that other black businesses were also hurt by desegregation. "All along Dowling Street were black businesses, black movie theaters, and shops. Blacks didn't own them, but they were managing them for white owners. When integration came, a lot of the blacks were forced out of business. If you went into the motel business when blacks couldn't stay at the Holiday Inn, then you did okay with a small place. People knew who you were and where you were located. But with integration you couldn't compete with the Holiday Inns, and that put you out of business or turned your motel into a hot sheet place. Integration was not always positive for black business. It forced some changes, but created new problems at the same time it created new opportunities."[49]

During the late 1960s and early 1970s, Benny Joseph did do "some commercial work for white photographers," although they only contacted him when "they were interested in getting something done real cheap. They had a client and didn't want to spend a lot of money. So they'd call me, but when I asked for more work, they never called back." Interactions of this kind discouraged Joseph from pursuing contracts and assignments from white-owned businesses. He was, however, able to restructure his own business successfully, and after losing his contracts for school photography, he began doing more studio and location work.

"I put my efforts into the black community," Joseph recalls. "People didn't have a lot of extra money for photographs in those days, but I could take a group picture and sell everybody a print because nobody had photographs of themselves. Cameras were not as available as they are today. The photograph had greater significance then as well."[50] Not only was the photograph a record of an event for an individual, it conferred social identity on its owner.

The photographs in this book have been selected from a collection of more than ten thousand negatives in preparation for the first touring exhibition of Joseph's work.[51] When I first met him in 1983, Joseph had recently closed his studio at 2305 Blodgett Street. His negatives were packed in numerically ordered paper envelopes in boxes that were stacked on the floor of his studio. Many of the negatives, however, were out of order and some had been misplaced or lost. Joseph did not keep written records but had a basic card file in which the names of his clients were arranged alphabetically and assigned negative numbers. Some of the envelopes were marked with the date the photographs were made, although most were undated. Joseph's conservation efforts were minimal. Some negatives were scratched or damaged. Negatives were stacked one on top of another in the envelopes, and they were often filed with the contact prints he made to show his clients. There were no vintage prints other than those portraits Joseph had made of his own family. The quality of these prints became the standard that was followed in the printing of both the exhibition and the plates for the book.[52]

In editing and printing the negatives, I worked closely with Joseph over a period of five years to identify those images which displayed the greatest lucidity of content, design, composition, and control over tonal values. The photographs in the book encompass the years from the mid-1950s to 1976. The Speedgraphic 4x5 camera he used during this period produced what Joseph considered his best work. In the 1970s Joseph switched to the 2¼x2¼ format and later to 35mm. He says, "I made better pictures with the Speedgraphic. I never did like the smaller format, but I had to use it for economic reasons. Four-by-five film became too expensive."[53]

Joseph estimates that 85 percent of his work over the course of his career was school portraiture; 5 percent, studio walk-in trade; and 10 percent, location assignments. Given the routinized methods of his portraiture, to show the broad range of Joseph's photography, I have placed greater emphasis in the book on his location work, which shows more variation in subject matter, composition, and style.

Joseph's studio photographs of musicians (such as Lightnin' Hopkins, Gatemouth Brown, Junior Parker, Johnny Brown, Don Wilkerson, Joe Hinton, and Little Frankie Lee) are representative of his style of portraiture and have been included because of their historical importance. The careers of these musicians have been well documented, but the photographs themselves are relatively unknown. Joseph poses his subjects the way they performed. He says, "I would ask them to go through their act. I wanted to help them pose by having them do what they normally did, some gesture or expression. I didn't talk too much. I'm a man of few words with a small vocabulary."[54]

In his location work Joseph focuses on the relationship of people to each other and to the environment in which they lived, worked, and performed. He says, "Anytime an organization, a newspaper, or a radio station would send me out to take a picture, they wanted to see the crowds. They wanted to see lots of people in it."[55] *In his photographs of performers like BB King and Mahalia Jackson on stage, he includes the interaction and response of the audience. In photographing Thurgood Marshall and Martin Luther King, Jr., Joseph shows "as much as possible about where and how they made their speeches. During the civil rights period the church was a place where politics and religion came together."*[56]

Generally, Joseph's location photographs were done on assignment. He was called to photograph a wide range of community-centered and newsworthy events, including political rallies, social club functions, concerts, advertising promotions, high school graduations, and car wrecks. In addition,

Joseph says, "It was fairly common in the 1950s for people to want to have photographs made of their deceased relatives, embalmed and ready for viewing at the funeral home or church."[57]

In some instances, however, Joseph worked "on a hustle." He remembers, "I used to go to the Eldorado Ballroom and other places. When I'd walk in, people would come up to me and say, 'Mr. Joseph, do you have your camera?' And I'd say, 'Yeah, it's down in the car.' People would be partying and they'd want their pictures made. At the teen hops the kids would plead with me. 'Take my picture! Take my picture!' I had no idea that these pictures would be anything other than snapshots. I might have asked them, 'Well, what am I going to do with it?' And they probably told me, 'I want it, I want it,' but they wouldn't get it unless they paid me first and I mailed it to them."[58]

While it could be argued that Joseph's collective work is not definitive of the early years of rhythm and blues, when seen together his photographs make a personal photographic statement that reveals the power of the music and its personalities in Houston culture. These photographs are representative of a generation that grew to maturity in the 1950s and 1960s, and they evoke a vibrant sense of African American life during a critical juncture in the history of the country.

The Photography of

BENNY JOSEPH

Plate 1

BB King

Plate 2   Club Matinee

Plate 3

Plate 4

Della Reese

Plate 5

Paul Monday

Plate 6   **Teen Hop**

Plate 7

Mahalia Jackson

Plate 8   KCOH Home Show Parade

Plate 9   **Martin Luther King, Jr.**   *31*

Plate 10

Barbara Jordan

Plate 11   **NAACP Regional Meeting**

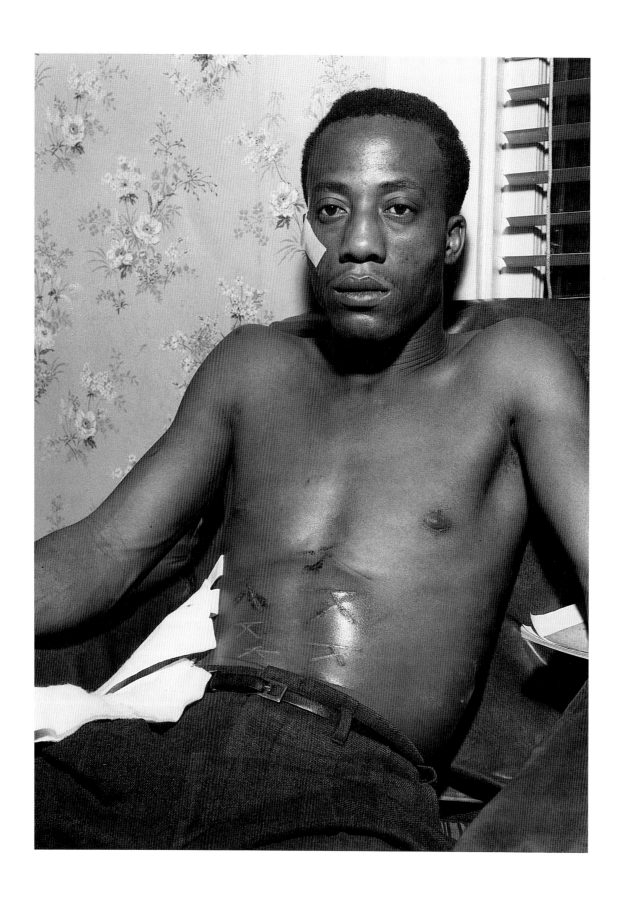

Plate 12   **Felton Turner**   34

Plate 13 **Thurgood Marshall**

Plate 14   **Carter Wesley**   36

Plate 15   **Lawrence Burdine, Leo Lachner, BB King**

Plate 17 Double Bar Ranch

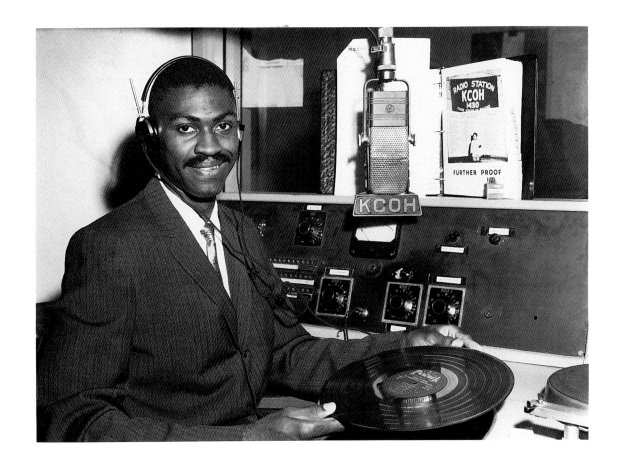

Plate 18   **Travis Gerner**

Plate 19   **Don Robey**

Plate 20   **Don Robey Awards**

Plate 21　　　　　　　　**Reverend Cleophus Robinson**　　　　　　　*43*

Plate 22   **Don Robey Hunting Trip**

Plate 23   **Clifton Smith**

Plate 24   **Remote Broadcast**

Plate 25   **KCOH Promotion**   47

Plate 26   **KCOH Disc Jockey**

Plate 27   **Teen Hop**

Plate 28 **Daddy Deepthroat, Perry Cain**

Plate 29   **Skipper Lee Frazier**

Plate 30   KCOH Remote Broadcast

Plate 31   Sam "Lightin'" Hopkins

Plate 32 **Clarence ''Gatemouth'' Brown**

Plate 33

"Junior" Parker

Plate 34   **John Browning**

Plate 36   **Eddie Vinson**   *58*

Plate 37   **Don Wilkerson**   *59*

Plate 38   **Albert Collins**   *60*

Plate 39   **Lester Williams**   *61*

Plate 40 **Buddy Ace**

Plate 43   **Toni Williams**   *65*

Plate 44

Little Frankie Lee

Plate 45   **Benny Joseph's Home**

Plate 47   **Kindergarten Graduation**

Plate 48   **Debutante Ball**   *70*

Plate 49

Children Dancing

Plate 51   ROTC Ball   73

Plate 53   **Cassius Clay**

Plate 54   Hansworth Car Wreck

Plate 55   **Deceased Baby**

Plate 56   **Easter Mass**

Plate 57   **Dance Contest Winners**

Plate 58   **Alma Jo Springs**

NOTES

1. Interview with Johnny Copeland, January 11, 1989.

2. For a more detailed discussion of the early history of the blues and the regional differences in style and form, see Paul Oliver, *Blues Off the Record* (Hippocrene Books, 1984), and *Songsters and Saints* (Cambridge University Press, 1984), Leroi Jones, (Imamu A. Baraka) *Blues People* (Morrow, 1963), David Evans, *Big Road Blues* (University of California Press, 1981), Bruce Bastin, *Red River Blues* (University of Illinois Press, 1986), Jeff Todd Titon, *Early Downhome Blues* (University of Illinois Press, 1979), Barry Lee Pearson, *Sounds So Good To Me* (University of Pennsylvania Press, 1984), and Robert Palmer, *Deep Blues* (Viking Press, 1981).

3. Robert Dixon and John Godrich, *Recording the Blues, 1902-1943* (Stein & Day, 1970). For more information, see Chris Albertson, *Bessie* (Stein & Day, 1982), and Daphne Duval Harrison, *Black Pearls: Blues Queens of the 1920s* (Rutgers University Press, 1988).

4. See Tony Heilbut, *The Gospel Sound* (Simon & Schuster, 1971), and Charlie Gillette, *Sound of the City* (Pantheon, 1970).

5. Helen O. Dance, *Stormy Monday: The T-Bone Walker Story* (Louisiana State University Press, 1987).

6. Ross Russell, *Jazz Style in Kansas City and the Southwest* (University of California Press, 1971), pp. 80-83, 101-111, 229-31.

7. Interview with Mariellen Shepphard, October 14, 1984.

8. Alan Govenar, *Meeting the Blues* (Taylor Publishing, 1988), pp. 57-59, 165-200, 201-233.

9. Govenar, pp. 75-140. "Houston Jump," 1946-51, "Krazy Kat KK 7406, liner notes by Bruce Bastin (1982), "Texas R&B, 1949-1952," Krazy Kat KK 7418, liner notes by Bruce Bastin (1983), "Houston Shuffle, 1955-1966," Krazy Kat KK 7425, liner notes by Bruce Bastin (1984).

10. Interview with Evelyn Johnson, January 29, 1989.

11. "Gatemouth Brown, The Original Peacock Recordings," Rounder 2039, liner notes by Dick Shurman (1983). "Gatemouth Brown, The Duke-Peacock Story," Vol. 1, Ace CHD 161.

12. Interview with Evelyn Johnson, January 26, 1989. For more information on the history of the Peacock Record Company, see Galen Gart and Roy C. Ames, "Taking My Chances: Don Robey and the Bronze Peacock," *Blues and Rhythm* (May 1989), No. 44, pp. 4-6, and Mike Leadbitter, *Nothing but the Blues* (Oak Publications, 1971).

13. Interview with Evelyn Johnson, February 8, 1989.

14. Heilbut, pp. 79-80.

15. Arnold Shaw, *Honkers and Shouters* (Collier Books, 1986), pp. 479-80.

16. Interview with Evelyn Johnson, January 29, 1989.

17. Govenar, p. 95. For more information, see Charles Sawyer, *BB King: The Authorized Biography* (Quartet Books, 1980).

18. Shaw, pp. 480-81. "A Memorial to Johnny Ace," Ace CH 40, liner notes by Dzondira Laisac.

19. Shaw, pp. 484-86. See also Peter Guralnick, *Lost Highway* (Vintage Books, 1982), pp. 68-91, and Charles Keil, *Urban Blues* (University of Chicago Press, 1966), pp. 114-142. "Earl Forrest Featuring the Beale Streeters," Ace CH 220, liner notes by Ray Topping (1987), "Bobby Bland, Blues in the Night," Ace CH 132, liner notes by Philip Chevron (1985), and "Bobby Blue Bland, Woke Up Screamin' " Ace CH 41, liner notes by Ray Topping (1981).

20. Interview with Bobby Bland, July 4, 1989.

21. Shaw, p. 479. "Big Mama Thornton, Quit Snoopin' Round My Door," Ace CH 170, liner notes by Ray Topping (1986).

22. Shaw, pp. 486-88. "Little Junior Parker and the Blue Flames," Ace CH 42.

23. "Lyons Avenue Jive," Ace CHD 171, liner notes by Ray Topping (1986), "Strutting at the Bronze Peacock," Ace CHD 223, liner notes by Ray Topping (1987), "Peacock Chicks and Duchesses," Ace CHD 233, liner notes by Ray Topping (1988).

24. Interview with Evelyn Johnson, January 29, 1989.

25. Interview with Evelyn Johnson, February 8, 1989.

26. Interview with Evelyn Johnson, January 26, 1989.

27. Interview with Evelyn Johnson, January 23, 1989.

28. Interview with Huey P. Meaux, March 11, 1989.

29. Interview with Benny Joseph, June 16, 1989.

30. Interview with Benny Joseph, July 22, 1989.

31. Interview with Benny Joseph, April 12, 1985.

32. Interview with Benny Joseph, June 16, 1989.

33. Interview with Benny Joseph, May 15, 1989.

34. For more information on the history of early African American photographers in Houston, see Dannehl M. Twoumy, "Into the Mainstream: Early Black Photographers in Houston," *Houston Review*, IX:1, pp. 39-48. Twoumy points out that early black photographers in Houston worked outside the central business area and that the location of their studios put them at a disadvantage with both black and white patrons, who were attracted to centrally located, white photographic studios.

35. Interview with Benny Joseph, September 3, 1988.

36. Interview with Alvia Wardlaw, October 15, 1988.

37. Interview with Alvia Wardlaw, October 16, 1988.

38. Interview with Benny Joseph, February 12, 1989.

39. Interview with Alvia Wardlaw, October 16, 1988.

40. Interview with Alvia Wardlaw, October 16, 1988.

41. Interview with Joe Hughes, March 23, 1988.

42. Interview with Alvia Wardlaw, October 16, 1988.

43. Interview with Francis Williams, October 17, 1989. For more information on the civil rights period in Houston, see Cary D. Wintz, "Blacks," in Fred R. von der Mehden, *The Ethnic Groups of Houston* (Rice University Press, 1984), p. 34, and Chandler Davidson, *Biracial Politics* (Louisiana State University Press, 1972).

44. Interview with Benny Joseph, June 16, 1989.

45. Interview with Benny Joseph, June 16, 1989. For more information, see *Houston Post* (March 9, 1960), Section 1, p. 1, *Houston Post* (March 17, 1960), Section 4, p. 3, and *Houston Informer* (March 19, 1960), p. 1.

46. Interview with Benny Joseph, September 3, 1988.

47. Interview with Benny Joseph, April 12, 1985.

48. Interview with Benny Joseph, September 3, 1988.

49. Interview with Skipper Lee Frazier, October 15, 1988.

50. Interview with Benny Joseph, June 16, 1989.

51. The exhibition, "The Photography of Benny Joseph," was curated by Alan Govenar and produced by Documentary Arts, Inc., in Dallas with the assistance of the Center for Study of Southern Culture at the University of Mississippi and made possible in part by grants from the Texas Commission on the

Arts and the National Endowment for the Arts through the Southern Arts Federation.

Tyler Museum of Art, January 14–April 16, 1989

Barker Texas History Center, May 12–June 25, 1989

Carver Museum, June 4–25, 1989

University Museums, University of Mississippi, July 8–August 13, 1989

Hughes–Trigg Student Center, Southern Methodist University, September 1–24, 1989

African American Heritage Museum of Houston, February 10–March 10, 1990

52. The prints were made by Ron Evans in consultation with Alan Govenar and Benny Joseph. The contemporary selenium-toned gelatin silver prints reflect the original printing style of the selenium-toned bromide prints, which were made at the time the negatives were created.

53. Interview with Benny Joseph, May 15, 1989.

54. Interview with Benny Joseph, April 12, 1985.

55. Interview with Benny Joseph, July 22, 1989.

56. Interview with Benny Joseph, June 16, 1989.

57. Interview with Benny Joseph, July 22, 1989.

58. Interview with Benny Joseph, April 12, 1985.

SELECTED BIBLIOGRAPHY

Chris Albertson, *Bessie* (Stein & Day, 1982).

Bruce Bastin, *Red River Blues* (University of Illinois Press, 1986).

Chandler Davidson, *Biracial Politics* (Louisiana State University Press, 1972).

Robert Dixon and John Godrich, *Recording the Blues, 1902-1943* (Stein & Day, 1970).

David Evans, *Big Road Blues* (University of California Press, 1981).

Galen Gart and Roy C. Ames, "Taking My Chances: Don Robey and the Bronze Peacock," *Blues and Rhythm* (May 1989), pp. 4-6.

Alan Govenar, *Meeting the Blues* (Taylor Publishing, 1988).

Peter Guralnick, *Lost Highway* (Vintage Books, 1982).

Houston Informer (March 19, 1960), p. 1.

Houston Post (March 9, 1960) Section 1, p. 1.
——(March 17, 1960) Section 4, p. 3.

Sheldon Harris, *Blues Who's Who* (Da Capo, 1983).

Daphne Duval Harrison, *Black Pearls: Blues Queens of the 1920s* (Rutgers University Press, 1988).

Tony Heilbut, *The Gospel Sound* (Simon & Schuster, 1971).

Leroi Jones (Imamu A. Baraka), *Blues People* (Morrow, 1963).

Charles Keil, *Urban Blues* (University of Chicago Press, 1966).

Lawrence W. Levine, *Black Culture and Consciousness* (Oxford University Press, 1977).

Mike Leadbitter, *Nothing but the Blues* (Oak Publications, 1971).

——and Neil Slaven, *Blues Records, 1943-1970*, 2nd ed., Vols. 1&2 (London: Record Information Services, 1987).

Living Blues, Nos. 1-86 (Center for the Study of Southern Culture, University of Mississippi, 1970-1989).

Paul Oliver, *Songsters and Saints* (Cambridge University Press, 1984).

——, *Blues Off the Record* (Hippocrene Books, 1984).

Robert Palmer, *Deep Blues* (Viking Press, 1981).

Barry Lee Pearson, *Sounds So Good To Me* (University of Pennsylvania Press, 1984).

Ross Russell, *Jazz Style in Kansas City and the Southwest* (University of California Press, 1971).

Arnold Shaw, *Honkers and Shouters* (Collier Books, 1978).
——as *Black Popular Music in America* (Schirmer Books, 1984).

Jeff Todd Titon, *Early Downhome Blues* (University of Illinois Press, 1979).

Dannehl M. Twoumy, "Into the Mainstream: Early Black Photographers in Houston," *(Houston Review*, IX:1, pp. 39-48).

Cary D. Wintz, "Blacks," in Fred R. von der Mehden, *The Ethnic Groups of Houston* (Rice University Press, 1984).

LIST OF PLATES

1. BB King at City
   Auditorium
   Houston, 1962/537
   Gelatin Silver print
   11" x 14"
   1988

2. Club Matinee
   Houston, 1957
   Gelatin Silver print
   14" x 11"
   1988

3. Couple Dancing
   26 Men Social Club
   Eldorado Ballroom
   Houston, 1962/760
   Gelatin Silver print
   11" x 14"
   1988

4. Della Reese
   Houston, n.d./6170
   Gelatin Silver print
   11" x 14"
   1988

5. Paul Monday
   Houston, n.d./1825
   Gelatin Silver print
   11" x 14"
   1988

6. Teen Hop, Eldorado
   Ballroom
   Houston, 1964
   Gelatin Silver print
   14" x 11"
   1988

7. Mahalia Jackson
   Houston, n.d./6170
   Gelatin Silver print
   11" x 14"
   1988

8. KCOH Home Show
   Parade
   Houston, n.d.
   Gelatin Silver print
   14" x 11"
   1989

9. Martin Luther King, Jr.
   Houston, n.d./495
   Gelatin Silver print
   11" x 14"
   1989

10. Barbara Jordan
    Houston, 1964/992
    Gelatin Silver print
    11" x 14"
    1988

11. NAACP Regional
    Meeting
    Houston, n.d./1642
    Gelatin Silver print
    14" x 11"
    1988

12. Felton Turner
    Houston, 1960
    Gelatin Silver print
    11" x 14"
    1989

13. Thurgood Marshall
    Houston, n.d./2046
    Gelatin Silver print
    11" x 14"
    1988

14. Carter Wesley
    Houston, n.d./1895
    Gelatin Silver print
    11" x 14"
    1989

15. Lawrence Burdine
    Leo Lachner, BB King
    Houston, ca. 1955
    Gelatin Silver print
    14" x 11"
    1988

16. Clifton Smith
    Diamond L Ranch
    Houston, n.d./1825
    Gelatin Silver print
    11" x 14"
    1988

17. Double Bar Ranch
    Houston, n.d./1825
    Gelatin Silver print
    11" x 14"
    1988

18. Travis Gerner
    KCOH Disc Jockey
    Houston, n.d./1907
    Gelatin Silver print
    14" x 11"
    1988

19. Don Robey
    If It's Not a Hit, I'll
    Eat My Hat
    Houston, 1957/649
    Gelatin Silver print
    14" x 11"
    1988

20. Don Robey, Awards
    Ceremony
    Pilgrim Temple,
    Houston, n.d./649
    Gelatin Silver print
    14" x 11"
    1988

21. The Reverend
    Cleophus Robinson
    Peacock Recording
    Studios
    Houston,
    ca. 1956/649
    Gelatin Silver print
    11" x 14"
    1988

22. Don Robey, Deer
    Hunting Trip
    Houston,
    ca. 1959/649
    Gelatin Silver print
    14″ x 11″
    1988

23. Clifton Smith
    KCOH Disc Jockey
    Houston,
    ca. 1958/1907
    Gelatin Silver print
    14″ x 11″
    1988

24. Remote Broadcast
    Gladys "Gigi" Hill
    KCOH Disc Jockey
    Davidoff
    Supermarket
    Houston, n.d./1907
    Gelatin Silver print
    14″ x 11″
    1988

25. KCOH Promotion
    Davidoff
    Supermarket
    Houston, n.d./1907
    Gelatin Silver print
    11″ x 14″
    1988

26. Unidentified KCOH
    Disc Jockey
    Houston, n.d./1907
    Gelatin Silver print
    14″ x 11″
    1988

27. Teen Hop, Eldorado
    Ballroom
    Houston, 1964
    Gelatin Silver print
    14″ x 11″
    1988

28. Daddy Deepthroat
    Perry Cain
    KCOH Disc Jockey
    Record Giveaway
    Houston, n.d./1907
    Gelatin Silver print
    14″ x 11″
    1988

29. Skipper Lee Frazier
    KCOH Disc Jockey
    Go-Go Girls
    Houston, 1965/7
    Gelatin Silver print
    14″ x 11″
    1988

30. KCOH Remote
    Broadcast
    Houston, 1960/1907
    Gelatin Silver print
    14″ x 11″
    1988

31. Sam "Lightin'"
    Hopkins
    Houston, 1972
    Gelatin Silver print
    11″ x 14″
    1988

32. Clarence
    "Gatemouth" Brown
    Houston, n.d./1337
    Gelatin Silver print
    11″ x 14″
    1989

33. "Junior" Parker
    Houston, 1964/1202
    Gelatin Silver print
    11″ x 14″
    1988

34. John Browning
    Houston, n.d./1238
    Gelatin Silver print
    11″ x 14″
    1988

35. Johnny Brown
    Houston, 1963/73
    Gelatin Silver print
    11″ x 14″
    1988

36. Eddie Vinson
    Houston, n.d./6497
    Gelatin Silver print
    11″ x 14″
    1988

37. Don Wilkerson
    Houston, 1964/610
    Gelatin Silver print
    11″ x 14″
    1988

38. Albert Collins
    Houston, 1965/44
    Gelatin Silver print
    11″ x 14″
    1988

39. Lester Williams
    Houston, n.d./861
    Gelatin Silver print
    11″ x 14″
    1989

40. Buddy Ace
    Houston, n.d./3255
    Gelatin Silver print
    11″ x 14″
    1988

41. O.V. Wright
    Houston, 1964/1776
    Gelatin Silver print
    11″ x 14″
    1988

42. Joe Hinton
    Houston, 1963/74
    Gelatin Silver print
    11″ x 14″
    1988

43. Toni Williams
    Houston, 1965/1238
    Gelatin Silver print
    11″ x 14″
    1988

44. Little Frankie Lee
    Houston, n.d./718
    Gelatin Silver print
    11″ x 14″
    1988

45. Benny Joseph's
    Home
    3106 Carlisle
    Houston, 1957/146
    Gelatin Silver print
    14″ x 11″
    1988

46. May Festival
    Our Mother of
    Mercy Church
    Houston, n.d./1712
    Gelatin Silver print
    11″ x 14″
    1988

47. Kindergarten
    Graduation
    Houston, n.d.
    Gelatin Silver print
    14″ x 11″
    1988

48. Jack and Jill
    Debutante Ball
    Houston, n.d./284
    Gelatin Silver print
    11″ x 14″
    1988

49. Children Dancing
    St. Peter Clavier
    Mardi Gras
    Houston, ca. 1958
    Gelatin Silver print
    11″ x 14″
    1988

50. Coronation Ball
    Jack Yates High
    School
    Houston, 1958/174
    Gelatin Silver print
    11″ x 14″
    1988

51. Thanksgiving Game
    ROTC Ball
    Jack Yates High
    School
    Houston, 1958/174
    Gelatin Silver print
    11″ x 14″
    1988

52. Dr. Arthur Riddle
    Houston, n.d./2137
    Gelatin Silver print
    11″ x 14″
    1988

53. Cassius Clay
    KCOH Promotion
    Houston, n.d./7
    Gelatin Silver print
    14″ x 11″
    1988

54. Hansworth Car
    Wreck
    Houston, n.d./1853
    Gelatin Silver print
    14″ x 11″
    1988

55. Deceased Baby
    Houston, n.d./274
    Gelatin Silver print
    14″ x 11″
    1988

56. Easter Mass
    Our Mother of
    Mercy Church
    Houston, n.d./1712
    Gelatin Silver print
    14″ x 11″
    1988

57. Dance Contest
    Winners
    Eldorado Ballroom
    Houston, 1964
    Gelatin Silver print
    14″ x 11″
    1988

58. Alma Jo Springs
    United Negro
    College Fund Queen
    Houston, 1960/1628
    Gelatin Silver print
    14″ x 11″
    1988